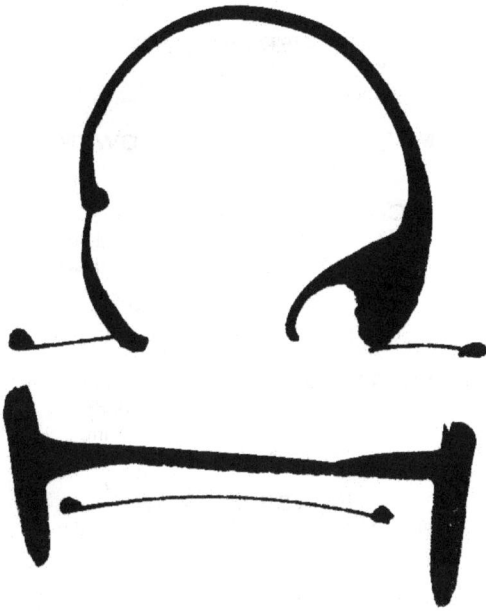

BY SABRINA MESKO

HEALING MUDRAS
Yoga for Your Hands
Random House - Original edition

POWER MUDRAS
Yoga Hand Postures for Women
Random House - Original edition

MUDRA - GESTURES OF POWER
DVD - Sounds True

CHAKRA MUDRAS DVD set
HAND YOGA for Vitality, Creativity and Success
HAND YOGA for Concentration, Love and Longevity

HEALING MUDRAS
Yoga for Your Hands - New Edition

HEALING MUDRAS - New Edition in full color:
Healing Mudras I. ~ For Your Body
Healing Mudras II. ~ For Your Mind
Healing Mudras III. ~ For Your Soul

POWER MUDRAS
Yoga Hand Postures for Women - New Edition

MUDRA THERAPY
Hand Yoga for Pain Management and Conquering Illness

YOGA MIND
45 Meditations for Inner Peace, Prosperity and Protection

MUDRAS FOR ASTROLOGICAL SIGNS
Volumes I. ~ XII.
MUDRAS for ARIES, TAURUS, GEMINI, CANCER, LEO, VIRGO,
LIBRA, SCORPIO, SAGITTARIUS, CAPRICORN, AQUARIUS, PISCES
12 Book Series

LOVE MUDRAS
Hand Yoga for Two

MUDRAS AND CRYSTALS
The Alchemy of Energy Protection

THE HOLISTIC CAREGIVER
A Guidebook for at-home care in late stage of Alzheimer's and dementia

MUDRAS

for

LIBRA

By Sabrina Mesko Ph.D.H.

The material contained in this book has been written for informational purposes and is not intended as a substitute for medical advice nor is it intended to diagnose, treat, cure, or prevent disease. If you have a medical issue or illness, consult a qualified physician.

A Mudra Hands™ Book
Published by Mudra Hands Publishing

Photography by Mara
Animal photography by Sabrina Mesko
Illustrations by Kiar Mesko
Cover photo by Mara

Printed in the United States of America

ISBN-13: 978-0615920924
ISBN-10: 0615920926

For all my Libra Friends

Table of Contents

THE MUDRA PRACTICE IS A
COMPLIMENTARY HEALING TECHNIQUE,
THAT OFFERS FAST AND EFFECTIVE
POSITIVE RESULTS.

MUDRAS WORK HARMONIOUSLY
WITH OTHER TRADITIONAL,
ALTERNATIVE AND COMPLEMENTARY
HEALING PROTOCOLS.

THEY HELP RESTORE DEPLETED
SUBTLE ENERGY STATES
AND OPTIMIZE THE PRACTITIONER'S
OVERALL STATE OF WELLNESS.

Mudras for LIBRA

SEPTEMBER 23 - OCTOBER 23

BODY
Kidneys

PLANET
venus

COLORS
pale blue, pink, green

ELEMENT
Air

STONES and GEMS
Sapphire, Jade

ANIMAL
Small reptiles

INTRODUCTION

Ever since I can remember, I have been fascinated by the never ending view of the stars in the sky and the presence of other mysterious planets. As a child I wondered for hours about where does the Universe end and when my Father explained the possibility that time and space exist in a very different way than we imagined, my mind went wild with possibilities. I was however quite skeptical about astrology in general until one day in my early youth, a dear friend introduced me to a true Master of Vedic Astrology. He quickly and completely diminished any of my doubts about how precise certain facts can be revealed in one's Celestial map.

It was as if an invisible veil had been removed, and I was granted a peek over to the other side. The astrologer also adamantly pointed out that nothing is written in stone and one's destiny has a lot of space to navigate thru. You can make the best of the situation if you know your given parameters. My fascination and use of astrological science continues to this day and compliments and enriches my work with other observation techniques that I use when consulting.

One is born with character aspects and potential for realization of mapped-out future events, but there is always a possibility that another road may be taken. This has to do with the choices we make. Free will is given to all of us, even though often the choices we have seem to be very limited. But still, the choices are always there, forcing us to consciously participate and eventually take responsibility for our decisions, actions, and consequences.

The science of Astrology has been around for millenniums and even though some people are still doubtful, I always remind them that there is no disputing the fact, that the Moon affects the high and low tide of our Oceans - hence our bodies consisting mostly of water are affected by planetary movements in many fascinating and profound ways. Even the biggest skeptic agrees with that fact.

The Love of the Universal Power for each one of us is unconditional, everlasting and omnipresent. No matter what kind of life-journey you have, it is the very best one designed especially for you, rest assured. And when you are experiencing life's various challenges and wishing for a smooth ride instead, keep in mind that a life filled with lessons is a life fulfilling its purpose. The tests you encounter in your daily life are your opportunities. The wisdom learned is your asset, and the experiences gained are your wealth. Your Spirit's abundance is measured by the battles you fought and how you fought them. Did you help others and leave this world a better place in any way? Your true intention matters more than you know.

Each one of us has a very unique-one of a kind celestial map placed gently, but firmly and irrevocably into effect at the precise time of our birth. There are certain aspects of one's chart that reveal possible character tendencies and predisposed behavior in regards to love, partnerships, maintaining one's health, pursuit of success and a way of communicating. The benefits of knowing and understanding the effects of your chart on various aspects of your life can be profound. It can help you understand and prepare ahead of time for certain circumstances that are coming your way, which increases the possibility of a better quality of life in general.

If you knew that a specific time period could be beneficial for your career wouldn't it be good to know that ahead of your plans? If you are aware that certain aspects of your physical constitution are predisposed to a weakness or sensitivity, wouldn't it be beneficial to pay attention and prevent a possible future health ailment?

If you can foresee that a certain time will be slower for you in achieving positive results, wouldn't it be wise to use that time for preparation for a more fortuitous timing? How many times have you attempted to pursue a dream of yours that just didn't seem to want to happen? And when you were completely exhausted and disillusioned, the fortunate opportunity presented itself, except now you were tired, overwhelmed and had no energy or enthusiasm left. Having such information ahead of time would offer you the chance to save your energy during quiet, less active time, so that when your luck is more likely, you can seize the opportunity and make the most of it. Since writing my first books on Mudras a while ago, my work has expanded into many different areas, however I always included Mudras into my new ventures. When I designed International Wellness and Spa centers, I included Mudra programs to share these beneficial techniques with a wide audience. I included Mudras into my weekly TV show and guided large audiences thru practice on live shows.

Mudras will forever fascinate me and I have been humbled and excited how many practitioners from around the world have written me, grateful to have these techniques and most importantly really experiencing positive effects in time of need. Therefore it has been a natural idea for me to combine these two of my favorite topics and create a series of Mudra sets for all twelve Astrological signs.

The Mudras depicted in this book are specifically selected for the astrological sign of Aries with intention to help you maximize your gifts and soften the challenges that your celestial map contains.

It is important to know that each astrological chart - celestial map-contains information that can be used beneficially and there are no "bad signs" or "better sings". Your chart is unique as are you. By gaining information, knowledge and understanding what the placements of the planets offer you, your path to self knowledge is strengthened.

I hope this book will attract astrology readers as well as meditation and yoga practitioners and help you utilize the beneficial combination of both these fascinating techniques. Knowledge will help you experience the very best possible version of your life. The biggest mystery in your life is You. Discover who you are and enjoy the journey.

And remember, no matter what life presents you with, don't forget to smile and keep a happy heart. With each experience gained you are spiritually wealthier for it. And that my friend, stays with you forever.

The wisdom gained is eternally imprinted in your soul.

Blessings,

Sabrina

MUDRAS

Mudras are movements involving only fingers, hands and arms. Mudras originated in ancient Egypt where they were practiced by high priests and priestesses in sacred rituals. Mudras can be found in every culture of the world. We all use Mudras in our everyday life when gesturing while communicating and when holding our hands in various intuitive positions. Mudras used in yoga practice offer great benefits and have a tremendously positive overall effect on our overall state of well-being. By connecting specific fingertips and your palms in various Mudra positions, you are directly affecting complex energy currents of your subtle energy body. As numerous energy currents run thru your brain centers, Mudras help stimulate specific areas for an overall state of emotional, physical and mental well being.

INSTRUCTIONS FOR MUDRA PRACTICE

YOUR BODY POSTURE
During the Mudra practice sit in an upright position with a straight spine, with both your feet on the ground or in a cross legged position. Comfort is essential so that you may practice undisturbed and focus on proper practice positions.

YOUR EYES
Keep your eyes closed and gently lightly lift the gaze above the horizon.

WHERE
For achieving best results of ideal Mudra practice it is essential that you find a peaceful place, without distractions. Once your Mudra practice is established, you can practice Mudras anywhere.

WHEN
You may practice Mudras at any time. Best times for practice are first thing in the morning and at bedtime. Avoid practicing Mudras on a full stomach, and after a big meal wait for an hour before practice.

HOW LONG
Each Mudra should be practiced for at least 3 minutes at a time. Ideal practice is 3 Mudras for 3 minutes each with a follow up short 3 minutes of complete stillness, peace and meditation or reflection.

HOW OFTEN
You may practice Mudras every day. Explore various Mudras by selecting a Mudra that fits your specific needs for any given day.

BREATH CONTROL
Proper breathing is essential for optimal Mudra practice. There are two main breathing techniques that can be used with your practice.

LONG DEEP SLOW BREATH
Slowly and deeply inhale thru your nose while relaxing and expanding the area or your solar plexus and lower stomach. Exhale thru the nose slowly while gently contracting the stomach area and pulling your stomach in. Pace your breathing slowly and notice the immediate calming effects. This breathing technique is appropriate for relaxation, inducing calmness and peace.

BREATH OF FIRE
Inhale and exhale thru the nose at a much faster pace while practicing the same concept of expanding navel area and contracting with each exhalation. Unless otherwise noted Mudras are generally practiced with the long slow breath.The breath of fire has an energizing, recharging effect on body and is to be used only when so noted.

Chakras

Along our spine, starting at the base and continuing up towards the top of your head, lie subtle energy centers-vortexes-called charkas, that have a powerful effect on the overall state of your health and well being.
The practice of Mudras profoundly affects the proper function of these energy centers and magnifies their power.

Our subtle energy body is highly sensitive to outside sensory stimuli of sound, aromas, visuals and outside electric currents that constantly surround us. Frequencies that permeate specific locations may attract or bother you. Perhaps you may feel eager to stay somewhere where the energy suits you and yet feel suffocated when the environment does not agree with you. We are all sensitive to energies, but some of us feel them more than others.

A positive blend of energies with another person can create a magnet-like effect, whereas another person's negative unharmonious subtle energy field subconsciously pushes you away.

By leading healthy lives and optimizing the proper function of charkas, you empower your subtle energy bodies adding strength to your physical body, mind and spirit. Destructive behavior like addictions and abuse weakens your Auric field and "leaks" your vital energy. By maintaining a healthy Aura-energy field, you can fine-tune your natural capacity for "sensing" places, situations and people that compliment your energy frequency.
In a state of "clean energy" you achieve capacity for high awareness and become your own best guide.

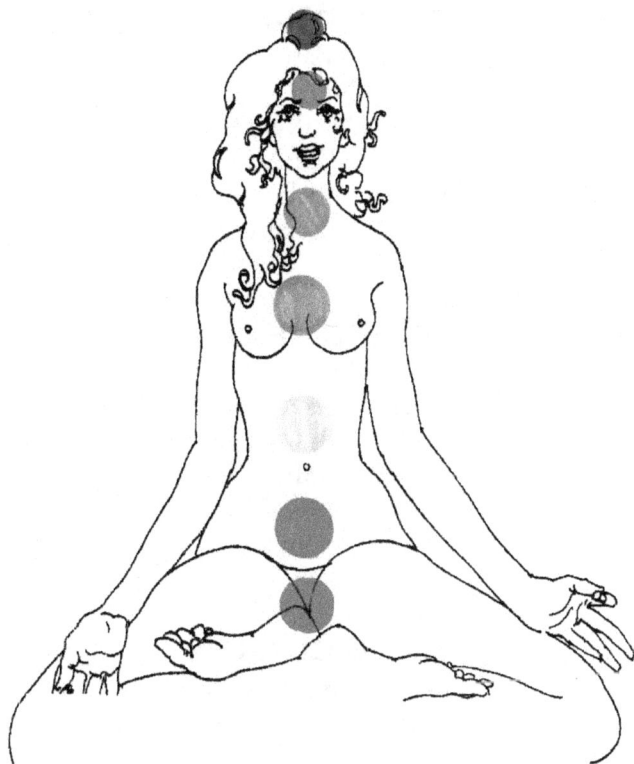

CHAKRAS IN THE BODY

Base Chakra: Foundation
Second Chakra: Sexuality
Third Chakra: Ego
Fourth Chakra: Love
Fifth Chakra: Truth
Sixth Chakra: Intuition
Seventh Chakra: Divine Wisdom

FIRST CHAKRA
LOCATION: Base of the spine
GLAND: Gonad
COLOR: Red
REPRESENTS:
Foundation, shelter, survival,
courage, inner security, vitality

SECOND CHAKRA
LOCATION: Sex organs
GLAND: Adrenal
COLOR: Orange
REPRESENTS:
Creative expression, sexuality,
procreation, family

THIRD CHAKRA
LOCATION: Solar plexus
GLAND: Pancreas
COLOR: Yellow
REPRESENTS:
Ego, intellect, emotions of fear and anger

FOURTH CHAKRA
LOCATION: Heart
GLAND: Thymus
COLOR: Green
REPRESENTS:
All matters of the heart, love,
self–love, compassion and faith

FIFTH CHAKRA
LOCATION: Throat
GLAND: Thyroid
COLOR: Blue
REPRESENTS:
Communication, truth,
higher knowledge, your voice

SIXTH CHAKRA
LOCATION: Third Eye
GLAND: Pineal
COLOR: Indigo
REPRESENTS:
Intuition, inner vision, the Third eye

SEVENTH CHAKRA
LOCATION: Top of the head - Crown
GLAND: Pituitary
COLOR: White and Violet
REPRESENTS:
The universal God consciousness,
the heavens, unity

NADIS

Your subtle energy body contains an amazing network of electric currents called Nadis. There are 72.000 energy currents that run throughout your body from toes to the top of your head as well as your fingertips. These channels of light must be clear and vibrant with life force for your optimal health and empowerment. With regular Mudra practice you can open, clear, reactivate and re-energize your energy currents.

Your Hands and Fingers

While practicing Mudras you are magnifying the effects of the Solar system on your physical, mental and spiritual body. Each finger is influenced by the following planets:

THE THUMB - MARS

THE INDEX FINGER - JUPITER

THE MIDDLE FINGER - SATURN

THE RING FINGER – THE SUN

THE LITTLE FINGER - MERCURY

MANTRA

Combining the Mudra practice with appropriate Mantras magnifies the beneficial effects of these ancient self-healing techniques.

The hard palate in your mouth has 58 energy meridian points that connect to and affect your entire body.

By singing, speaking or whispering Mantras, you touch these energy points in a specific order that is beneficial and has a harmonious and healing effect on your physical, mental and spiritual state.

The ancient science of Mantras helps you reactivate nadis, magnifies and empowers your energy field, improves your concentration and stills your mind.

About Astrology

The word Horoscope originates from a Latin word ORA–hour and SCOPOS–view. One could presume that Horoscope means "a look into your hour of birth". The precise moment of your birth determines your celestial set-up.

An accurate astrological chart can reveal most detailed aspects of your life, your character, your gifts, your future possible events, challenges that await you, lucky events that are bestowed upon you, and your outlook for happy relationships, successful careers, accomplishments, health and many possible variations of life events. I say possible, because your decisions will determine the outcome.

There are 12 signs in the Zodiac and your birth-day reflects the position of your Sun sign. The specific positions of other planets in your chart are calculated considering the precise moment-hour and minute and of course location of your birth. The birth time will reveal your Rising or Ascending sign, which will further determine other essential facts of your chart.

The constant transitional movements of the Planets affect each one of us differently, a time that may be difficult for some may prove supremely lucky for another and yet we are interconnected by mutual effects of continuous planetary movements. Nothing is standing still, the changes are ongoing. On a different note, a few slow moving planets connect us in other ways, as they keep certain generations under specific aspects and influences. We are all inseparable and in continuous motion.

There are numerous fascinating ways to use astrology and there is no doubt that the constant motion of all these powerful and majestic Planets in our Solar system affect each and every one of us differently. Astrology can be used as an additional tool to help you continue progressing on the mysterious life journey of self discovery and self-realization.

Remember, the power of decision is yours as is the responsibility for consequences. Make peace with your doubts, pursue your dreams and relish in results.

When the outcome is less than what you expected, learn to pick yourself up and continue on, wiser with knowledge you gained, that alone being a good reason for remaining optimistic. When the outcome surpasses your expectations, well, then you will know what to do…mostly take a breath, smile, and enjoy the moment.

Your Sun Sign

There are 12 signs in the Zodiac. The day of your birth determines your Sun-sign. Most often this is the extent of average person's knowledge and interest in astrology. However, the other aspects in the astrological chart are equally as important and need to be taken into consideration. In this book your main guide is your Sun sign's dispositions, tendencies, weaknesses and gifts. Certainly there are endless combinations of charts and your Sun sign alone will not reveal the complete picture of your celestial map.

For more detailed information and reflection about your chart, you need to know your ascending-rising sign.

Your Ascending-Rising Sign

Your rising sign, also known as the ascendant, reflects the degree of ecliptic rising over the eastern horizon at the precise moment of your birth. It reveals the foundation of your personality. That means that even if you have the same birthday with someone else, your time of birth would create completely different aspects and influences in your chart. No two people are alike. You are one of a kind and so is everyone else. However, you may have some strong similarities and timing aspects that will be often alike. Your rising sign also reveals the basis of your chart and House placements. Your rising sign determines and is in your first house. There are 12 Houses and each depicts precise in-depth information about all aspects of your physical life, emotional make and character tendencies. It is incredibly complex and fascinating. Regarding your Mudra practice in combination with your Astrological Sign, it would be beneficial to know also your Rising sign and apply Mudras that empower your Rising sign as well. For example; if your Sun sign is Aries, but your rising sign is Libra-it would be most beneficial to practice Mudra sets for both signs.

How to use this book

In each book of the *Mudras for the Astrological Signs* series, you will find Mudras for different astrological signs that will help you in most important areas of your life: Health, Love, Success, and Overcoming your challenging qualities. We all have them, as we also all have gifts. This book is specific for the sign of Aries. You may change your Mudra practice daily as needed, and keep in mind, that certain habits or tendencies need a longer time to adjust, change, and improve. Be patient, kind, and loving towards yourself.

Mudras for Transcending Challenges

Each one of us has a few character tendencies or weaknesses that are connected to our astrological chart. To help you transcend, overcome and redirect these challenges into your beneficial assets, you can use the Mudras in this chapter.

Mudras for Health and Beauty

Each astrological sign rules certain areas of your body. The Mudras in this chapter will help you strengthen your physical weaknesses while maintaining a healthy body, and a beautiful, vibrant appearance.

Mudras for Love

The Mudras in this chapter will help you understand your love temperament, your expectations, your longings and how to attract the optimal love partner into your life. It is most beneficial to know how others perceive you in the matters of the heart. It will also help you understand your partner and their astrologically influenced love map.

Mudras for Success

The Mudras in this chapter will offer you tools to present yourself to the world in your optimal light. Often one is confused in which direction to turn or where their strength lies. Mudras will help you focus and remember your essential creative desires, help you gain self-confidence and inner security to recognize your desired and destined path. If you know what you want, and your purpose is harmonious for the better good of all, your success is within reach.

MUDRAS
for TRANSCENDING
CHALLENGES

MUDRA
FOR GUIDANCE

Being the symbol of balance you have an uncanny capacity to weight the options. When someone asks for help and advice, you will lay out all the facts and help them see the picture clearly. That is a very special gift, yet when it comes to you it may prove a bit more challenging. Weighing your options too long can turn into indecisiveness and making yourself vulnerable to distracting outside influences. You will need this Mudra to help guide you thru your hesitation and indecisive moments.

CHAKRA: 7

COLOR: White

Sit with a straight spine. Place your hands together in front of your chest. Little fingers are pressed together to form a cup. Palms are facing towards the sky. Leave a very small opening between the sides of the little fingers. Gently focus your eyes towards the tip of your nose towards the palms. Have a clear question. Hold for three minutes, relax, be calm and wait for a clear answer.

BREATH: Long, deep and slow into your palms.

MUDRA FOR
FACING FEAR

You do not like being left alone and a very social. People enjoy your company and you are quite popular. However, when it comes to revolutionary causes or putting up a fight, you prefer the diplomatic route and will prefer to play it safe and won't insist on a confrontation. You enjoy peace and will always feel a duty to help preserve that. To help you overcome challenging moments of unavoidable conflict, practice this Mudra and remain untouchable and calm.

CHAKRA : 3, 7

COLOR: Yellow, violet

MANTRA:

NIRBHAO NIRVAIR AKAAL MORT
(Fearless, Without Enemy,
Immortal Personified God)

Sit with a straight back. Bend your right elbow and lift the arm up to the level of your face. Face your palm outward, as if taking a vow. Bring your left arm in front of your navel, palm facing up. Concentrate on energy being received into your palms and hold for at least three minutes. Relax and be still.

BREATH: Long, deep and slow.

MUDRA FOR CONTENTMENT

In order to get what you want, you need to know what you want in the first place. If you do not address the order of things this way, you will feel discontent and often jealous of others. Knowing yourself is the key element to achieve happiness on all levels and in all areas of your life. If you do not actively participate in the decision making process and would rather stay on the fence instead of commit to a side, it would be most beneficial if you would be able to make peace within yourself with the consequences. Take responsibility for your indecisiveness and remain content with the outcome. This Mudra will help you achieve that.

CHAKRA : 7

COLOR: Violet

MANTRA:

SARE SA SA SARE SA SA SARE HARE HAR
(God Is Infinite in His Creativity)

Sit with a straight back and lift your hands in front of your stomach area. Connect the thumb and middle finger of the right hand and the thumb and the little finger of the left hand. Relax the rest of the fingers and hold your hands a few inches apart, palms up. Hold for three minutes, then make fists with both hands and relax. Position is reversed for men.

BREATH: Long, deep and slow.

MUDRAS
for HEALTH
and BEAUTY

MUDRA for VITALITY
and Letting GO

When you feel yourself unnecessary dwelling on a certain event or circumstance, you need to " live and let go". Decision has been made and there is no need to carry unnecessary negative emotions with you. Regular exercise is important for your health as well as a healthy diet. Your sign rules the kidneys, so keeping toxins to a minimum is imperative. That includes mental and emotional restlessness. Retain your vital energy and use it for positive, harmonious and happy frame of mind.   For best results practice this Mudra regularly.

CHAKRA : 1, 2

COLOR: Red, orange

MANTRA:

SAT NAM
(Truth is God's Name, One in Spirit)

Sit with a straight back and place your fists in front of you, palms facing up. Concentrate on your base chakra. Sit tall and attempt to stretch as if trying to get taller. Be aware of the ground underneath you and the life force of the earth.

BREATH: Long, deep and slow.

MUDRA for
Protecting Your HEALTH

You like a comfortable and easy going pace in life. What is important for you to remember is the need for a healthy diet, so do not let your sweet tooth get the best of you. Inactivity could cause you to gain some extra pounds that you don't need, keeping active and productive will help you keep that under control. In matters of general health pay attention to what really best suits you and do not be too gullible or easily influenced to go in the wrong direction. The best option is for you to keep an all around healthy lifestyle and take some time to find that perfect balance for yourself. After all, balance is your speciality.

CHAKRA : All color

COLOR: All color

MANTRA:

OM
(God in His Absolute State)

Sit with a straight back. Bend your right elbow and lift your left hand up, palm facing out. The index and middle fingers are pointing up; the rest are curled with the thumb over them. Hold your left hand in the same Mudra with the two stretched fingers touching your heart. Hold for three minutes.

BREATH: Inhale for ten counts, hold the breath for ten counts, and exhale for ten counts. Pace yourself comfortably, relax and be still.

MUDRA FOR
LOWER SPINE

Your sign rules the kidneys and lower back therefore it is wise to pay extra attention to these areas and keep them as healthy and vital as possible. Be disciplined and remember that preserving your health is the best investment ever made-make that extra effort and keep a wise diet and conflict free living environment at work and especially at home. You need harmony in every possible way. Practice this Mudra to help you strengthen your vulnerable areas and prevent a potential challenging situation. Harmonize your life, begin with the base-your spine. Make this Mudra a part of your morning routine.

CHAKRA : 1, 2

COLOR: Red, orange

MANTRA:

OM
(God in His Absolute State)

Sit with a straight spine and make fists with both hands. Leave the thumbs stretched out and hold the hands in front of you. The palms are facing the ground and the thumbs are directed toward each other. Keep the fists strong and feel the energy pulsating in your palms. After three minutes relax your hands and rest.

BREATH: Long, deep and slow.

MUDRAS
for LOVE

MUDRA FOR
RELEASING ANXIETY

Falling in love is a blessing that happens when destiny calls. You really do not have to make a decision there, for it is made for you. However, once in love, eventually decisions to move forward will have to be made and this will be a challenge for you. You are very harmonious with your partner and there will never be any arguing, except when you need extra proof that they love you unconditionally. Then you may test them, which is of course very unproductive. Instead, practice this Mudra and release your inner anxiety, wether it has to do with getting engaged, married or simply moving in together. Give it a go and you'll see, a new harmonious environment will be established and you will be even happier than before.

CHAKRA : 4, 5, 6

COLOR: Green, blue, indigo, violet

MANTRA:
HARKANAM SAT NAM
(God's Name Is Truth)

Sit with a straight spine. Bend your elbows and raise your arms so your upper arms are parallel to the ground and extended out to the sides. Your hands are at the level of your ears, fingers spread wide and pointing to the sky. Start rotating your hands back and forth pivoting at the wrists. Practice for three minutes and be persistent. You will go thru a period when it seems difficult, but when you overcome that moment, the practice will be easy.

BREATH: Long, deep and slow.

MUDRA FOR OPENING YOUR HEART

You are a great romantic and will have no trouble mesmerizing your partner with that perfect environment you created. You may only have to fight within yourself first to get to that point. Sitting on the fence about making the first move won't pay off. So get your courage together and take a chance. This Mudra will help you open your heart to this new love, so you will recognize and experience the true meaning of unconditional. It means; no conditions, no negotiations, and not indecisiveness. Here you are, now jump.

CHAKRA : 4

COLOR: Green

MANTRA:
SAT NAM
(Truth is God's Name, One in Spirit)

Sit with a straight spine and lift your hands in front of your heart with palms and fingers open as if creating a cup. Keep all the fingers stretched and feel healing energy pouring into your fingertips and the area of your heart.

BREATH: Long, deep and slow.

MUDRA FOR OPENING
YOUR CROWN

Finding your life partner is very important to you. You may be very successful, engaged in much socializing, and surrounded by many friends. Yet, until your true love appears you will feel lonely. Being alone is something you dislike and avoid at all costs. In order to attract the right partner into your life, you need to be receptive to the Universal energy. By opening your connection to the ultimate source, you will find yourself drawn to a place and time where the perfect partner awaits. It could be around the corner or on another continent. It does not matter, what is important is that you do not resist your destiny. This Mudra will help you open your receptive sensory capacity and follow the magical path.

CHAKRA : 7

COLOR: VIOLET

MANTRA:
OM
(God in His Absolute State)

Sit with a straight spine. Lift your hands above your head, all fingers kept apart as if you were holding a crown on your head. Keep the arms at this level and fingers stretched the entire practice. Visualize a stream of bright white light pouring into the crown of your head and filling your entire body with healing light.

BREATH: Long, deep and slow.

MUDRAS
for SUCCESS

MUDRA FOR
INNER SECURITY

Your natural God given beauty is something that you rely on.
You may work in fashion, beauty, design and love luxury and
all that it offers. If for a moment you feel a bit unsure about
that aspect, an insecurity could spoil the best of times for
you. Develop and rely on your other qualities that you are
gifted with; your charming, romantic, easy going nature that
is very attractive and appealing. This Mudra will help you
dispel   those clouds of insecurity so that you will remain
the sunshine of the crowd.

CHAKRA: 3, 4

COLOR: Yellow, green

MANTRA:

AD SHAKTI AD SHAKTI

(I Bow to the Creator's Power)

Sit with a straight back, place your hands in reversed prayer pose: hands touching back to back at the level of your heart and solar plexus. Hold the pose for one and a half minutes, then repeat with the palms pressed together in a prayer pose.

BREATH: Long, deep and slow.

MUDRA FOR
SELF - CONFIDENCE

When during discussions you are not clearly voicing your opinion, it may appear that you are not secure within yourself. The truth may be that you just want to avoid taking sides, since you dislike any kind of confrontation or conflict. To help you overcome this trait which will not always serve in your best interest, practice this Mudra. It will help you participate in discussion with confidence as your opinion does matter and is valuable. Engage your strong diplomatic talents and achieve peace within the group. Be confident that you can do that, for it is your hidden talent and gift.

CHAKRA : 3, 6

COLOR: Yellow, indigo

MANTRA:

**EK ONG KAR SAT GURU PRASAD
SAT GURU PRASAD EK ONG KAR**
(The Creator Is the One That Dispels Darkness
and Illuminates Us by Hs Grace)

Sit with a straight back. Lift your hands up to the level of your solar plexus with elbows bent to the sides. Bend the middle, ring, and little fingers and touch them back to back. Extend the index fingers and thumbs and press them together. The thumbs are pointed toward you and the index fingers away from you.

BREATH: Long, deep and slow.

MUDRA FOR
DIMINISHING WORRIES

Since you like luxury and a comfortable life, you need to make plenty of money to make it all happen. This creates of course a certain level of pressure for pursuing and maintaining the lifestyle that comes with a high price. However, a top executive job presents a certain level of loneliness which you won't like. Perhaps it would be best to find a happy medium and compromise. So you may have to sacrifice a few fancy perks, but it will help you sleep peacefully at night. Make a good plan of your wants, needs and sacrifices, then it will be easier for you to find that golden balance. When worry overcomes you, practice this Mudra and remember that every problem has a solution. It is all within your reach.

CHAKRA: 4, 5, 6

COLOR: Green, blue, indigo

Sit with a straight back. Bring your hands in front of your chest with the palms facing up. The sides of the little fingers and inner sides of the palms are touching. Now bring the middle fingertips together, perpendicular to the palms. Extend the thumbs away from the palms. Hold and keep the fingers stretched as little antennas for energy.

BREATH: Long, deep and slow.

ABOUT THE AUTHOR

SABRINA MESKO   PH.D.H. is an International and Los Angeles Times bestselling author of the timeless classic *Healing Mudras - Yoga for your Hands* translated into fourteen languages. She authored over twenty books on Mudras, Mudra Therapy, Mudras and Astrology, Holistic Caregiving, Spirituality and Meditation techniques.

Sabrina holds a Bachelors Degree in Sensory Approaches to Healing, a Masters in Holistic Science, a Doctorate in Ancient and Modern Approaches to Healing, and a Ph.D.H in Healtheoloyy from the American Institute of Holistic Theology. She is board certified from the American Alternative medical Association and American Holistic Health Association. She has been featured in media outlets such as The Los Angeles Times, CNBC News, Cosmopolitan, the cover of London Times Lifestyle, The Discovery Channel documentary on Hands, W magazine, First for Women, Health, Web-MD, Daily News, Focus, Yoga Journal, Australian Women's weekly, Blend, Daily Breeze, New Age, the Roseanne Show and various international live television programs. Her articles have been published in world-wide publications. She hosted her own weekly TV show educating about health, well being and complementary medicine. She is an executive member of the World Yoga Council and has led numerous international Yoga Therapy educational programs. She directed and produced her interactive double DVD titled *Chakra Mudras* - a Visionary awards finalist.

Sabrina also created award winning international Spa and Wellness Centers and is a motivational keynote conference speaker addressing large audiences all over the world. She is the founder of Arnica Press, a boutique Book Publishing House. Her mission is to discover, mentor, nurture and publish unique authors with a meaningful message, that may otherwise not have an opportunity to be heard. She is the founder of world's only online Mudra Teacher and Mudra Therapy Education, Certification and Mentorship program, with her certified therapists spreading these ancient teachings in over 28 countries around the world.

www.SabrinaMesko.com

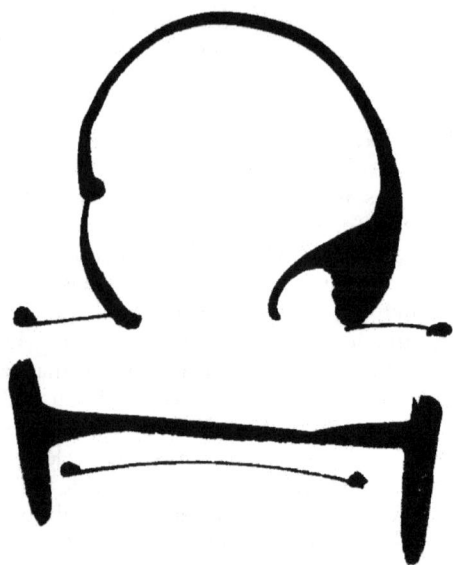

www.ingramcontent.com/pod-product-compliance
Lightning Source LLC
Chambersburg PA
CBHW071431040426
42445CB00012BA/1337